Christians Unite!

SAVING THE USA

Commit your works to the Lord and
Your plans will be established.

(Proverbs 16:3)

By Ernest D. Skipper

Christians Unite!

✝

Vision for the USA

God's Kingdom on earth growing, Americans once again embracing Him as the foundation of our lives, and He is honored in all bodies of government.

ISBN-13: 978-0-9904661-0-9

Table of Contents

Dedication

I dedicate this book to all of the military personnel who served to win and protect our freedom. Closer to home, I dedicate this work to my:

- Fifth great-grandfather Rev Nathan Skipper who fought in the Revolutionary War at the battles of Brandywine, Germantown and Monmouth.

- Family's WWII veterans:
  (Past) Father-in-law Elbert Gadberry, who fought on Omaha Beach and his twin brother, Delbert, who was killed when shot down over Germany
  (Current) Father-in-law Woodrow Wolfe, who fought in the African Theater.

Never forget, without these men willing to give it all we wouldn't be free today.

My actions to "Save the USA" are dedicated to the protection of our freedoms which are under attack. I want my grandchildren –Megan, Jack, Aidan, Andrew, Brandon, and Matthew – to live free, achieving God's plan for them. I pray they will remember the millions who gave much for their freedom and will also fight to protect it.

✞

... I urge you, brethren, by the mercies of God, to present your bodies a living and holy sacrifice, acceptable to God, which is your spiritual service of worship. And do not be conformed to this world, but be transformed by the renewing of your mind, so that you may prove what the will of God is, that which is good and acceptable and perfect.

(Romans 12:1-2)

Acknowledgements

Most importantly, I thank God for the Bible – the greatest book ever written – and His saving grace. He never gave up on me.

I acknowledge the assistance of my wife, Vanna, for her encouragement and time spent reading and correcting my many mistakes.

I also thank the following ministers for their many sermons which helped shape my understanding of God's word. I know I still (and will always) have much to learn:

- Steve Viars, Faith Church, Lafayette, Indiana
- Jim McCarty, First Baptist Church, Port Charlotte, Florida
- John MacArthur, Grace Community Church, Sun Valley, California
- S. Lewis Johnson, Believers Chapel, Dallas, Texas
- David Jeremiah, Shadow Mountain Community Church, San Diego, California

I thank Billy Falling, Minister and Author, Chula Vista, California for his "Fundamental Doctrines of the Christian Faith" Bible study course and his book *The Political Mission of the Church*. This book should be required reading for every Christian and student of American history.

Foreword

Ernest Skipper adds his voice to the growing chorus of Americans asking for a return to America's foundations. In this booklet, he takes us on a fast track from problems to solution. Three things cannot be denied in this educational primer:

- God's word
- America's Christian heritage
- The original intent of this country's Constitution

In one paragraph Skipper quotes George Washington, and in the next, the Apostle Paul. He strips back the dark curtain of Saul Alinski's *Rules for Radicals* (the handbook for liberals), and quotes Thomas Jefferson's personal letter mentioning the separation of church and state.

Theologians may be quick to split hairs over terms. Get over it. As the generations who have presided over our country's decline, this is no time to continue fighting over eschatology or definitions. The bottom line: we are at war and the enemy is within, nurtured due to the Christian church's default.

America's bright future lies with new revolutionaries like Ernest Skipper. He has identified our problems and lends his life, fortune, and sacred honor to saving our country.

May this work of sacrifice and love spread throughout the United States of America.

- Billy Falling
Keynote speaker and founder of the
Christian Voters' League

Chapter 1

Just Imagine

Imagine it is November 4, 2020, the morning after the national election. The sun is shining, the air is cool and fresh. The news is streaming on every TV channel: the conservatives maintained the presidency and control of both houses of congress with a clear path to restoring conservative values throughout the country. The networks are in shock and disbelief, wondering how this happened. Why did the people turn against the liberal, humanist, feel good, do-whatever-you-want platform and vote for the conservative mandate?

The highlights of the campaign platform:
- ✓ Constitution honored as USA foundation
- ✓ Balanced budget amendment
- ✓ Repeal of Roe v. Wade
- ✓ Accurate American history taught K-12
- ✓ Marriage between one man and one woman
- ✓ Secure the borders
- ✓ God accepted and honored in our government
- ✓ Flat income tax

And yes, all of this builds on the great improvements achieved since the conservatives gained control in the 2016 elections. This is now a clear endorsement for widespread change throughout all branches of government and the public education system. Once again the truth of American history will be taught in our public schools and universities. Yes, there is hope for America!

Credit for this shift in public opinion and prevailing attitude of the American people goes to the Christians across the country who finally woke up and said "enough is enough." They joined together to advance God's kingdom on earth and save the USA. There is great optimism across the country as God's blessing shines once more on America. The most shocking statement made by the media is: God must be in control!

It is good to think about what might be. Could it become reality instead of a wishful daydream? The answer is "Yes" if we unite as a Christian body to advance God's kingdom here on earth, allowing God's return to our government and schools.

If it is possible to achieve this kind of change, why are we complacent about the current state of the economy and the prevalent culture? There are too many un- and underemployed, families living on the streets, children going hungry, overwhelmed soup kitchens, and food pantries short on food. Where will it end? How can it be fixed? Or does anyone really care?

Back in the real world, today's just another day: thousands of babies aborted; homosexual marriage laws moved forward; Christian organizations targeted by government agencies; national debt accelerated at approximately $2.2 million per minute. (5 year avg. 2009 - 2013)[1] Are we blinded to this?

There is a better way. Join us. We can make 2020 a year for a great victory in Christ.

"Here is my servant whom I have chosen,
the one I love, in whom I delight;
I will put my Spirit on him,
and he will proclaim justice to the nations.

He will not quarrel or cry out;
no one will hear his voice in the streets.

A bruised reed he will not break,
and a smoldering wick he will not snuff out,
till he has brought justice through to victory.

In his name the nations will put their hope."

(Matthew 12:18-21)
New International Version (NIV)

---

[1] http://www.usgovernmentdebt.us/us_deficit

✟

For I am convinced that neither death, nor life, nor angels, nor principalities, nor things present, nor things to come, nor powers, nor height, nor depth, nor any other created thing, will be able to separate us from the love of God, which is in Christ Jesus our Lord.

(Romans 8:38-39)

Chapter 2

A Christian Nation

It is easy to prove America was founded as a Christian nation if we know where to look for evidence. From documents written by the Pilgrims in 1620 we find these words:

> "Having undertaken, for the glory of God and advancement of the Christian Faith..."[2]

In 1643 these words,

> "We all came unto these parts of America with one and the same end and aim, to advance the Kingdom of our Lord Jesus Christ and to enjoy the liberties of the gospel in purity and peace."[3]

In their faith lay the seeds of democracy for America which gave birth to the Constitution and the Bill of Rights.[4]

The founding fathers believed in God and the truths of the Bible. Their fight was with the King of England who resisted God's law and refused their petitions. They had a choice. They followed God.

---

[2] Kate Caffrey, The Mayflower, p. 115.
[3] Billy Falling, Christian Political Science, p. 44
[4] Billy Falling. The Political Mission of the Church, p. 12

In a communication to the people, The Massachusetts Bay Company said:

> "Resistance to tyranny becomes the Christian and social duty of each individual. Continue steadfast, and with a proper sense of your dependence on God...nobly defend those rights which heaven gave."[5]

From noted statesman, Patrick Henry:

> "It cannot be emphasized too strongly or too often that this great nation was founded, not by religionists, but by Christians; not on religions, but on the gospel of Jesus Christ!"[6]

There were fifty-five men involved in the writing of the Constitution and most claimed to be men of God. There were 31 Episcopalians, 16 Presbyterians, 8 Congregationalists, 2 Dutch Reformed, 2 Methodists, 2 Roman Catholics and 2 Lutherans, and 3 Quaker..[7] It is certain God was directing the development of this foundational document.

> "One detail that is never mentioned is that in Washington, D.C. there can never be a building of greater height than the Washington Monument. With all the uproar about removing the Ten Commandments, etc., this is worth a moment or two of your time.

> On the aluminum cap, atop the Washington Monument in Washington, D.C., are displayed two words: Laus Deo.

---

[5] Bancroft, History VII, p.229.

[6] David Barton, The Myth of Separation, back cover

[7] http://www.adherents.com/gov/Founding_Fathers_Religion.html, p. 1

No one can see these words. In fact, most visitors to the monument are totally unaware they are even there and for that matter, probably couldn't care less.

Once you know Laus Deo's history, you will want to share this with everyone you know. These words have been there for many years; they are 555 feet, 5.125 inches high, perched atop the monument, facing skyward to the Father of our nation, overlooking the 69 square miles which comprise the District of Columbia, capital of the United States of America.

Laus Deo! Two seemingly insignificant, unnoticed words. Out of sight and, one might think, out of mind, but very meaningfully placed at the highest point over what is the most powerful city in the most successful nation in the world.

So, what do those two words, in Latin, composed of just four syllables and only seven letters, possibly mean? Very simply, they say 'Praise be to God!'"[8]

The United States was founded as a Christian nation upon Judeo-Christian principles. Denial of the fact cannot dispel it.

Why do so many challenge and attack our rich heritage? They seem to hate what Jesus Christ stands for and they hate Him. Since we are His, they also hate us.

> *"If the world hates you, you know that it has hated Me before it hated you. If you were of the world, the world would love its own; but because you are not of the world, but I chose you out of the world, because of this the world hates you."*
>
> (John 15:18-19)

---

[8] http://www.john-michael.net/2011/04/laus-deo/

They know they are doing wrong. They simply don't want to be reminded, especially by the gospels. Their desire is to do anything which makes them happy and feels good at the moment. And they don't want us, Jesus, or anyone holding them accountable. There it is. That word. "Accountability." It is absent in the humanists' culture. Nothing is their fault; someone else did it or made them do it.

Let's be reminded of a prayer from George Washington,

"Let my heart, gracious God, be so affected with Your glory and majesty that I may... discharge those weighty duties which Thou requirest of me ...." Again. "I have called Thee for pardon and forgiveness of sins... for the sacrifice of Jesus offered on the cross for me. Thou gavest Thy Son to die for me; and hast given me assurance of salvation." [9]

What can we learn about George Washington, the father of our country, from this brief prayer? That he believed: 1) in the death, burial, and resurrection of Jesus Christ, 2) in personal accountability, 3) that he was a sinner needing God's forgiveness, 4) in the power of the Holy Spirit, 5) in the power of prayer, 6) in salvation through the blood of Jesus Christ, and 7) that he alone could not accomplish the task at hand.

It is no longer a wonder why he was a great leader and the father of our country. He was a great example for us to follow as we seek to save the USA.

---

[9] William Johnson, George Washington, The Christian, p. 23-28

Chapter 3

Today's Reality

God's wisdom is no longer sought or given a place in our federal government. We rely on the "wisdom" of sinful humans. We've boxed up the gospel of Jesus Christ and confined it to the church building. We sit on our couches and watch TV shows produced by an evil, corrupt culture. Our sense of what is *true* changed and is shaped to the worldview.

We worship other gods without realizing it, being spoon-fed these gods through commercials and programming. Many things occupy our time and cause us to take our eyes off of Jesus: sports, cars, vacations, food, movies, TV, drugs, alcohol, sex, porn, our homes, and accumulation of "stuff." These are examples of other gods if we become compulsive about them. Consider the money spent annually on:[10]

- Self-storage units: $24 billion
- Movies: $31 billion
- Porn: $14 billion

---

[10] *These are approximate numbers from various websites, such as http://www.selfstorage.org/ssa/content/navigationmenu/aboutssa/fact sheet/, and http://www.omgfacts.com/Sports/The-American-Sports-industry-is-worth-42/53738. They are used only for illustration.*

- TV: $66.8 billion
- Sports: $422 billion
- Alcohol (beverages) $189 billion
- Illegal drugs: $150 billion
- Fast food: $188 billion

These things are not all wrong or sinful, but once they become the driving force behind our activities and take our focus away from bringing glory to God, they become another god. This is a sin.

Let's look at one other statistical comparison of today's culture in America. The total GDP in America is $15.684 trillion[11]. If 10% of it were given to the church, the annual revenue would be $1.568 trillion. However, total church donations are only approximately $128.6 billion[12] – a mere .8%. Sadly, 2.7% is spent on sports! Sports are not bad. They are simply a reflection of something more important in our culture than our Christian faith.

Here are some of the most striking changes to the American culture caused by this moving away from God:

- Thousands of babies aborted/killed, daily
- A "free sex" life style
- Homosexual marriage
- The media "spinning" news
- The national debt exceeding the annual GDP[13]
- The unemployment rate misreported
- Food stamps accepted as the norm
- Billions given to hostile-to-U.S. nations

---

[11] http://www.tradingeconomics.com/united-states/gdp, pg. 1
[12] http://www.deseretnews.com/article/700217384/Church-donations growing-at-less-than-half-the-rate-of-overall-charitable-giving.html? pg. 1
[13] http://www.tradingeconomics.com/united-states/government-debt-to-gdp, p. 1

- Turning our back on Israel
- Christian organizations targeted by our government

Add to the list a sad precedence set in 2008: a president elected because of the color of his skin, good communication skills, and a promise of change; but with no experience or a clear understanding of who he is or where he came from.

All of this happened while the churches of Jesus Christ remained silent. And a political party ran on a platform of supporting abortion, homosexual marriage, free contraceptives for everyone, and expanding the role of federal welfare. They won. *Twice.*

What must God think about the nation He helped godly men establish just over two hundred years ago?

Our constitutional framework is threatened by the pen and the phone of the president. How do we protect our system of governance for the next 200 years?

In our republic, Congress writes the laws and the president enforces them when they pass. If a US president does not like a piece of legislation, he has one constitutional mechanism to destroy it: a veto. There is no process for him to *change* it or circumvent Congress. However, our president changes laws as if he were back in the Senate amending a bill. Unfortunately, we allow it.

Example: On July 12, 2012 the Obama Administration issued a bureaucratic edict declaring that state welfare bureaucracies would no longer need to comply with the work participation standards established in the 1996 welfare reform law. Under the new policy, all states and all TANF recipients could potentially be exempted from federal work requirements. This edict blatantly violated the intent and letter of the welfare reform legislation.[14]

---

[14] http://www.heritage.org/research/reports/2012/09/obamas-end-run-on-welfare-reform-part-two-dismantling-workfare, p. 2

Our president issues executive orders to weaken work requirements for welfare programs[15], halts enforcement of immigration laws[16], and has implemented a radical environmental regulatory scheme.

Most troubling is his directly undermining the separation of powers, a provision put in place to protect us from a government capable of infringing upon our rights.

Article II, Section 3 of the United States Constitution declares, the president "... shall take care that the laws be faithfully executed." Known as the Take Care Clause, the founders understood directives made by one branch of our government and not enforced by another render the lawmakers powerless in a republic.

When the president's legacy, the Affordable Care Act, passed, he waived or delayed parts of "his" legislation numerous times without congressional action.[17]

If we do not restore the separation of powers, the corruption of the current presidency will continue to threaten our individual rights and our republic.

How are we advancing His kingdom on earth and demonstrating love when we don't challenge the culture which is corrupting the USA?

---

[15] http://www.heritage.org/research/reports/2012/09/obamas-end-run-on-welfare-reform-part-two-dismantling-workfare, p. 1

[16] http://www.fairus.org/publications/president-obama-s-record-of-dismantling-immigration-enforcement, p. 1

[17] www.thealtantic.com/national/archieve/2013/07/delaying-parts-of-obamacare-blatantly-illegal-or-routine-adjustment/277873/, p. 1

✟

Commit your works to the Lord and your plans will be established.

(Proverbs 16:3)

"The fundamental basis of this nation's laws was given to Moses on the mount...If we don't have a proper fundamental moral background, we will finally end up with a totalitarian government which does not believe in rights for anybody except the State."

- Harry S. Truman

Chapter 4

What Happened

Separation of Church and State

Satan, the father of all liars, knows if you repeat untruths long enough, people will believe them. One example: The United States Constitution does not call for separating God out of our government. In fact, the term "separation of church and state" was not part of a congressional discussion. It was a term used by Thomas Jefferson in a private letter to a Baptist organization. He was clearly denying the possibility of a "state church," such as accepting Roman Catholicism or the Church of England as a national denomination to which all must belong.

To help us understand how liberal judges interpret words to serve their agendas, here is the text from Jefferson's letter to the Danbury Baptist church.

To: Danbury Baptist Association in the State of Connecticut

Gentlemen,

The affectionate sentiments of esteem and approbation which you are so good as to express towards me, on behalf of the Danbury Baptist association, give me the highest satisfaction. My duties dictate a faithful and zealous pursuit of the interests of my constituents, & in proportion as they are persuaded of my fidelity to those duties, the discharge of them becomes more and more pleasing.

Believing with you that religion is a matter which lies solely between Man & his God, that he owes account to none other for his faith or his worship, that the legitimate powers of government reach actions only, & not opinions, <u>I contemplate with sovereign reverence that act of the whole American people which declared that their legislature should "make no law respecting an establishment of religion, or prohibiting the free exercise thereof," thus building a wall of separation between Church & State</u>.

Adhering to this expression of the supreme will of the nation in behalf of the rights of conscience, I shall see with sincere satisfaction the progress of those sentiments which tend to restore to man all his natural rights, convinced he has no natural right in opposition to his social duties.

I reciprocate your kind prayers for the protection & blessing of the common father and creator of man, and tender you for yourselves & your religious association, assurances of my high respect & esteem.

> (signed) Thomas Jefferson Jan.1.1802
> [emphasis mine]

Isn't it amazing how one well-meaning sentence, written over two hundred years ago, could be twisted and used to destroy the work of our founders? We and our parents allowed this to happen, creating the humanist culture which denies the grace of Jesus Christ.

Even the US Supreme Court upholds the thought that "separation" was not in the minds of the founders. Justice William O. Douglas wrote the majority decision in the 1952 case of Zorach v. Clauson:

"The First Amendment, however, does not say that in every and all respects there shall be a separation of Church and State... Otherwise the state and religion would be aliens to each other - hostile, suspicious, and even unfriendly...Municipalities would not be permitted to render police or fire protection to religious groups. Prayers in our legislative halls; the appeals to the Almighty in the messages of the Chief Executive; these and all other references to the Almighty that run through our laws, our public rituals, our ceremonies would be flouting the First Amendment."

"We are a religious people whose institutions presuppose a Supreme Being...When the state encourages religious instruction...it follows the best of our traditions. For it then respects the religious nature of our people and accommodates the public service to their spiritual needs. To hold that it may not would be to find in the Constitution a requirement that the government show a callous indifference to religious groups. That would be preferring those who believe in no religion over those who do believe."[18]

After the Declaration of Independence was signed, Samuel Adams noted:

"We have this day restored the Sovereign, to Whom alone men ought to be obedient. He reigns in heaven and

---

[18] United States Supreme Court. 1952, Zorach v. Clauson, 343 US 306 307 312-314 (1952),

... from the rising to the setting sun, may His Kingdom come."[19]

On April 30, 1789, George Washington stood before a crowd of people in New York and took the oath of office becoming the first president of the United States of America. He took this oath with his hand placed directly on the Bible and understood this passage from Deuteronomy 28:

Now it shall be, if you diligently obey the LORD your God, being careful to do all His commandments which I command you today, the LORD your God will set you high above all the nations of the earth.

Being men of God, George Washington and the founding fathers pledged to govern accordingly. To accomplish this, godly men must be involved in government. Who else would understand obeying the Lord? They also understood the second part of Deuteronomy 28:

But it shall come about, if you do not obey the LORD your God, to observe to do all His commandments and His statutes with which I charge you today, that all these curses will come upon you and overtake you:

We removed God from our government and culture, supporting those who do not observe His commandments or statutes. God tells us what to expect, because He is in control of the consequences resulting from our decisions:

Cursed shall you be in the city, and cursed shall you be in the country.

Cursed shall be your basket and your kneading bowl.

---

[19] Falling, ibid., p. 45.

Cursed shall be the offspring of your body and the produce of your ground, the increase of your herd and the young of your flock.

Cursed shall you be when you come in, and cursed shall you be when you go out.

The Lord will send upon you curses, confusion, and rebuke, in all you undertake to do, until you are destroyed and until you perish quickly, on account of the evil of your deeds, because you have forsaken Me."

(Deuteronomy 28:16-20)

Churches preach a message, from Romans 13:1-3, that we should accept those in power, keep quiet, and stay in line:

Every person is to be in subjection to the governing authorities. For there is no authority except from God, and those which exist are established by God. Therefore whoever resists authority has opposed the ordinance of God; and they who have opposed will receive condemnation upon themselves. For rulers are not a cause of fear for good behavior, but for evil. Do you want to have no fear of authority? Do what is good and you will have praise from the same.

"Keeping quiet" is not God's plan! Our government was designed by conservative, godly men who were led by God through the process. They set up a system of checks and balances for a government of the *people,* by the *people* and for the *people.* They expected all of us to participate.

In Ephesians 6:12, Paul tells us:

For our struggle is not against flesh and blood, but against the rulers, against the powers, against the world forces of this darkness, against the spiritual forces of wickedness in the heavenly places.

How can our form of government and culture survive without godly men actively defending God's laws? John Quincy Adams said, as president:

> "The highest glory of the American Revolution was this, it connected in one indissoluble bond, the principles of civil government with the principles of Christianity."[20]

From George Washington, as he left office:

> "Of all the dispositions and habits which lead to political prosperity, Religion and Morality are indispensable supports ... And let us with caution indulge the supposition that morality can be maintained without religion. Reason and experience both forbid us to expect that national morality can prevail in exclusion of religious principle." [21]

With these thoughts in mind, it should be no surprise where we are today because the forces of darkness are in control of our government and culture. God told us, through Paul:

> *For the wrath of God is revealed from heaven against all ungodliness and unrighteousness of men who suppress the truth in unrighteousness, because that which is known about God is evident within them; for God made it evident to them. ...Professing to be wise, they became fools, and exchanged the glory of the incorruptible God for an image in the form of corruptible man ...exchanged the truth of God for a lie, and worshiped and served the creature rather than the Creator, who is blessed forever. Amen.*
>
> *For this reason God gave them over to degrading passions; for their women exchanged the natural function*

---

[20] Barton, ibid., back cover.
[21] William Johnson, ibid., p. 218.

for that which is unnatural, and in the same way also the men abandoned the natural function of the woman and burned in their desire toward one another, men with men committing indecent acts and receiving in their own persons the due penalty of their error.

...they are gossips, slanderers, haters of God, insolent, arrogant, boastful, inventors of evil, disobedient to parents, without understanding, untrustworthy, unloving, unmerciful; and although they know the ordinance of God, that those who practice such things are worthy of death, they not only do the same, but also give hearty approval to those who practice them.

(Romans 1:18-32)

Please take note of the last words of the final verse, **"...give hearty approval to those who practice them."** There you go!

People like the false teachers who tell them only what they want to hear. They are encouraged to feel comfortable in their sin. Preachers are popular when they don't ask too much of us and when they tell us our greed or lust might be good for us. But a true teacher of God speaks the truth, regardless of what the listeners want to hear.

Democrats and Republicans are not to blame. We – the Christian Churches and community – let this happen! Electing a Republican president and changing control of the Senate and Congress will not solve the problems. The root cause of our problem is: God has been removed from the American culture and our government.

By the grace of God and our actions, we will fix the problem.

✝

Therefore, to one who knows the right thing to do and does not do it, to him it is sin.

(James 4:17)

Chapter 5

Culture of Dependency

Dependency or personal accountability? This is the choice we must make quickly, because our nation is being "fundamentally transformed" into something our founders would not recognize as the United States. We must wake up and stand up for our individual liberties, and above all our freedom to worship God without interference from the government.

The original settlers arrived at Plymouth Rock in 1620. They came here for the freedom to worship God as they chose, not as those who ruled over them demanded. They took a great life-and-death gamble for a better future. They trusted in God for leadership, guidance, and protection.

Throughout the history of our great country, we have been blessed and the envy of nations around the world. Why? I believe because of the wisdom of our founding fathers, creating a government with a foundation built on these beliefs: One nation, under God, with liberty and justice for all. It is a government of the people, by the people and for the people. A great nation developed from this foundation, because millions of people accepted responsibility for their actions. They received the benefits from success, and heartaches from failure.

Our success is a blessing from God, having founding fathers with the wisdom to establish a government allowing for freedom of worship.

Unfortunately, for the past 100 years, a liberal movement has been destroying what made the U.S. great.

The bigger the government, the greater the dependency. With every new program providing a handout, the greater the dependency. With every tax break, the greater the dependency and on and on it goes. The more dependent we become on the government, the more likely we are to say "The government will take care of me. I don't worry about it.", or "The more kids I have, the more money I get!" Approximately 49 percent of the people in America enjoy all the greatness of our country, but don't pay any federal income tax.[22]

Dependency and greed. It's nothing more, nothing less, and at no time in the United States' history have we seen anything like it. Trillions we can't afford are being spent, and we let it happen right in front of us. It is a drug called money, and it leads to dependency.

The one most important responsibility of our federal government is protecting our country. Ironically, this is the one thing they refuse to do – secure our borders. Why? It is about creating another dependency group through welfare programs, gaining control over them, and yes, securing votes.

This is not about Democrats or Republicans, left or right wing, liberal or conservative. This is about the destruction of individual liberty; as Christians we are being led to slaughter like a flock of sheep, saying nothing. Most churches won't get involved for fear of losing their tax status -- another dependency.

We, as sane human beings, make decisions and take actions based on what we believe is true. Our concept of truth is formed from our life experiences. These incidents formed our habits,

---

[22] http://blog.heritage.org/2012/02/19/chart-of-the-week-nearly-half-of-all-americans-dont-pay-income-taxes/, p. 1

attitudes, beliefs, and expectations. As a result our comfort zone has been created that we live in. And it has been found that we don't let ourselves want what we don't think we can have or achieve.

But Moses said to God, "Who am I, that I should go to Pharaoh, and that I should bring the sons of Israel out of Egypt?"

(Exodus 3:11)

God asked Moses to step out of his comfort zone, and Moses offered many reasons why he should not. It is difficult to move away from the familiar, even when we are told it is for our own good (or the good of others).

Those with the money, power and influence (who are moving this darkness across America) seem to understand the principles of cognitive psychology and dependency. This appears to be their plan. When they are in the majority, it is difficult to remove them. However, their majority is fragile. There is still time to retake our country.

The challenge – faced by Christians since Jesus gave his life for our sins – is moving people from their comfort zone (no matter how painful the process may be) and toward accepting Jesus into their lives. It is difficult and fearful because it is unknown; it goes against their habits, attitudes, beliefs, and expectations. Once they make the commitment, it gets easier and a new "security blanket" forms. God is with them, through the Holy Spirit, helping them form new habits, attitudes, beliefs and expectations.

Today the government creates dependencies through government programs. Unions, AARP, ACCORN, NAACP, special interest groups, political action committees, and many other groups claim to represent our interests. Do they, or are they also creating a dependency?

This new American dependency mindset starts early. Many parents don't hold children accountable for right and wrong and schools often ignore behavior problems. As they grow older, government dependency programs step in and special interest groups create *more* dependency programs.

Could it be the first time someone needs "personal account-ability" is when accepting – or not – Jesus as their Lord and Savior? How difficult will it be for them to make that decision if someone else runs their lives?

Before all the government programs, the poor turned to God, church, and community for help. That's as it should be. But now the government through these programs demonstrates a desire to keep them from turning to God, church, and community. They want control and dependency for future votes and long-term power, and to rewrite the America which created the greatness we know.

These dependency programs are destroying the opportunity for greatness as God intended -- no different than a dependency on drugs or alcohol destroys opportunities for greatness. Church attendance is declining for younger people. Why? In my opinion, it is about dependency, right and wrong, and unwillingness to accept responsibility for their lives. Do whatever feels good at the moment! The Ten Commandments can't be taught or displayed. Whose fault is that? We and our parents let it happen! How much more will we take?

Remember the line "the devil is in the details?" I believe the devil is in the details and the foundation for all these dependency programs. Government programs are great for those who can't do, and should be continued; but those who *can* do should never be given a handout. They should be offered a hand up and only when necessary. Tax breaks and funding for businesses and organizations should never be considered permanent, but should be for short periods, and if necessary reapproved each year by congress.

I've heard a story about a family, on a farm in rural Missouri in 1960, receiving commodities: free food. This was a family with several children, which owned a farm, and appeared to be doing well. Someone asked how a family could swallow its pride and accept help from the government. How things have changed!

Christians must unite around a belief in accountability and individual liberties if we are to take back our government, a government founded on a belief in God, and a government of the people, by the people and for the people. God's second great commandment is revealed in Matthew 22:39;

You shall love your neighbor as yourself.

Can you stand before God and say you loved your neighbor as yourself and let this dependency culture grow? We can't let the evil forces of darkness chip away at our governmental foundation anymore.

> **This is not about the church taking over the government. This is about individuals saying enough is enough.**

"Our society strives to avoid any possibility of offending anyone – except God."

- Billy Graham

Chapter 6

The Great Killer

Almost exactly nine months after World War II ended, "the cry of the baby was heard across the land." More babies were born in 1946 than ever before: 3.4 million, 20 percent more than in 1945. This was the beginning of the "Baby Boom" generation. In 1947, another 3.8 million babies were born; 3.9 million were born in 1952; and more than 4 million were born every year from 1954 until 1964, when the boom finally tapered off. By then, there were 76.4 million "Baby Boomers" in the United States. They made up almost 40 percent of the nation's population.[23]

Do you wonder about the lasting impact we, as a generation, will have on America? How will we be judged by history fifty or a hundred years from now? Consider how much the world has changed since the 1950s, and how many of those transformations were caused by the now "60-somethings."

Most of our parents grew up in or most certainly were influenced by the Great Depression. They developed and held certain truths many of us don't share or understand. Some left school after the eighth grade to work and help their families. Fighting Germany and Japan, during World War II, shaped their belief system. Because of their fight for freedom, they earned the name

---

[23] http://www.bbhq.com/bomrstat.htm, p. 1

"the Greatest Generation." They fought the Nazi killing machine which executed approximately six million Jews and another five million selected people. These murders started in January 1933 and didn't end until May 1945. They killed, on average, nearly one million people per year. Think about that!

It was a horrible time for the Greatest Generation – our parents – who valued life, freedom, and hard work. They gave it all to provide us a better life. They believed they were stewards of this land and were charged with the responsibility of working to make it better for the next generation.

What happened? As we grew older, Boomers fought for social, economic and political equality and justice for disadvantaged groups: African-Americans, young people, women, homosexuals, American Indians, and Hispanics, for example. Student activists took over college campuses, organized massive demonstrations against the war in Vietnam, and occupied parks and other public places. Young people also participated in the wave of uprisings which shook American cities in the 1960s.

Others "dropped out" of political life altogether. "Hippies" grew their hair long, experimented with drugs, and, thanks to the newly-accessible birth control pill, practiced "free love." Some moved to communes.

Then the final straw: Roe v. Wade, January 22, 1973. It became legal, in the United States, for women to kill their unborn babies. Suddenly, it was alright to think of pregnancy as a disease to treat and destroy. Since January 1973, approximately 55.6[24] million babies have been killed in America through abortion. Every third baby conceived is murdered in the womb. Four thousand a day, 170 an hour! Planned Parenthood kills a baby every ninety-five seconds. We are murdering more people than Hitler's Nazi party did! Approximately 65% of the women who

---

[24] http://www.abort73.com/abortion_facts/us_abortion_statistics/, p. 1

have an abortion claim to be Christian.[25] An underage girl doesn't need parental approval to get an abortion at Planned Parenthood. Additionally we pay for abortions with our federal tax dollars! And we still have the nerve to sing "God Bless America." Should we just stand on the sideline and support a government that pays for the killing of human life?

The Bible says;

I formed you in the womb but before I formed you in the womb, I knew you.

(Jeremiah 1:5)

God weaves together the genetic code; He intimately sees the unformed baby and He guides the entire process. Clearly abortion is the killing of a human life which was created by God, for His glory.

Behold, children are a gift from the Lord.

(Psalm 127:3)

We say we are "… one nation under God…." How did we allow unrighteous judges on the Supreme Court to sanction these actions? Our parents' generation fought, and thousands died, to stop Hitler and we embrace the killing of human life as a woman's choice? May God have mercy on us!

In the 2012 Presidential campaign one party ran on the following platform and won.

Protecting a Woman's Right to Choose

"We strongly and unequivocally supports Roe v. Wade and a woman's right to make decisions regarding her pregnancy, including a safe and legal abortion, regardless of ability to pay. We oppose any and all efforts to weaken or undermine that right.

---

[25] http://www.abort73.com/abortion_facts/us_abortion_statistics/, p. 2

Abortion is an intensely personal decision between a woman, her family, her doctor, and her clergy; this is no place for politicians or government to get in the way."[26]

Freedom to Marry

"We support the right of all families to have equal respect, responsibilities, and protections under the law. We support marriage equality and support the movement to secure equal treatment under law for same-sex couples. We also support the freedom of churches and religious entities to decide how to administer marriage as a religious sacrament without government interference.

"We oppose discriminatory federal and state constitutional amendments and other attempts to deny equal protection of the laws to committed same sex couples who seek the same respect and responsibilities as other married couples. We support the full repeal of the so called Defense of Marriage Act and the passage of the Respect for Marriage Act."[27]

Not only have our political parties bought into this way of life, but thousands of churches have watered down God's word and support this immorality.

This will be the Baby Boomers' legacy unless we do something to correct a culture focused on "self-satisfaction."

> .... the Lord came to me saying, "Can I not, O house of Israel, deal with you as this potter does?" declares the Lord. "Behold, like the clay in the potter's hand, so are you in My hand, O house of Israel. At one moment I might speak concerning a nation or concerning a kingdom to uproot, to pull down, or to destroy it; if that nation against which I have spoken turns from its evil, I will relent concerning the calamity I planned to bring on

---

[26] Moving America Forward 2012 Democratic National Platform, p. 18.
[27] Moving America Forward 2012 Democratic National Platform, p. 18.

it. Or at another moment I might speak concerning a nation or concerning a kingdom to build up or to plant it; if it does evil in My sight by not obeying My voice, then I will think better of the good with which I had promised to bless it.

(Jeremiah 18:5-10)

The solution is clear! We can't fix everything by creating conflict, as is our normal humanly instinct. Jesus tells us:

Put your sword back in its place. All who use swords will be killed with swords.

(Matthew 26:52)

The mass media is part of the problem, using their power and resources to destroy us. Look at how they work to demolish the Tea Party and any other group speaking against the Washington establishment.

We must use a different approach that Jesus would have used.

"I don't believe there is a problem in this country or the world which could not be settled if approached through the teaching of The Sermon On the Mount."

- Harry S. Truman
33rd President

Chapter 7

The Liberal View
of the USA

The liberal agenda controls the Washington establishment. While it began in the early twentieth century with baby steps, liberalism became highly visible in the 60s and accelerated. Today, this movement is changing the fabric of our government. Maybe the most striking change in recent years is the national news media outlets "spinning" events to achieve their goals for our country (which includes turning it into a socialist state). It appears if those in control don't want a story released, it is held back. What a stark change from even 20 years ago!

Saul Alinsky (1909-1972) a community organizer, writer, and political activist wrote books titled *Reveille for Radicals* (1946) and *Rules for Radicals* (1971). *Rules for Radicals* is generally recognized as the handbook of modern day community organizing and was used by our current president.[28]

Alinsky was born in a Chicago slum to Russian Jewish immigrant parents, and these early conditions of poverty may have established his ideas and mode of action.[29]

---

[28]http://www.boston.com/bostonglobe/editorial_opinion/letters/articl es/2008/08/31/son_sees_fathers_handiwork_in_convention/, p. 1
[29] http://www.economicpolicyjournal.com/2013/04/hillary-clintons-

Community organizers are trained using the model outlined in Alinsky's *Rules for Radicals*. They also focus on "Relationships Built on Self Interest." As you read through these next few pages, remember President Obama's speeches during his first campaign. Chilling.

"Barack Obama's training in Chicago by the great community organizers is showing its effectiveness. It is an amazingly powerful format, and the method of my late father always works to get the message out and get the supporters on board. When executed meticulously and thoughtfully, it is a powerful strategy for initiating change and making it really happen. Obama learned his lesson well.

"I am proud to see that my father's model for organizing is being applied successfully beyond local community organizing to affect the Democratic campaign in 2008. It is a fine tribute to Saul Alinsky as we approach his 100th birthday."[30]

Now that we know the revolution's handbook, what can we learn about its contents as we proceed to hold them off and take back our nation? The following are quotes from *Rules for Radicals*:

"Lest we forget at least an over-the-shoulder acknowledgment to the very first radical: from all our legends, mythology, and history...the first radical known to man who rebelled against the establishment and did it so ef-

---

1969-thesis-on-saul.html, p1
[30] http://www.boston.com/bostonglobe/editorial_opinion/letters/articl es/2008/08/31/son_sees_fathers_handiwork_in_convention/, p. 1

fectively that he at least won his own kingdom -- Lucifer."[31]

"An organizer working in and for an open society is in an ideological dilemma to begin with, he does not have a fixed truth -- truth to him is relative and changing; everything to him is relative and changing... To the extent that he is free from the shackles of dogma, he can respond to the realities of the widely different situations..."[32]

"The third rule of ethics of means and ends is that in war the end justifies almost any means..."[33]

"From the moment the organizer enters a community he lives, dreams... only one thing and that is to build the mass power base of what he calls the army. Until he has developed that mass power base, he confronts no major issues.... Until he has those means and power instruments, his 'tactics' are very different from power tactics. Therefore, every move revolves around one central point: how many recruits will this bring into the organization, whether by means of local organizations, churches, service groups, labor unions, corner gangs, or as individuals."

"Change comes from power, and power comes from organization."[34]

---

[31] https://www.goodreads.com/author/quotes/59314.Saul_D_Alinsky, p. 1

[32] Rules for Radicals, A Practical Primer for Realistic Radicals, Saul Alinsky, pp.10-11

[33] Saul Alinsky, Rules for Radicals, A Practical Primer for Realistic Radicals, p.29.

[34] Saul Alinsky, Rules for Radicals, A Practical Primer for Realistic Radicals, p.113

"The first step in community organization is community disorganization. The disruption of the present organization is the first step toward community organization. Present arrangements must be disorganized if they are to be displaced by new patterns.... All change means disorganization of the old and organization of the new."[35]

Alinsky established 13 tactical rules for community organizers:

1. Power is not only what you have, but what the enemy thinks you have.

2. Never go outside the expertise of your people.

3. Whenever possible, go outside the expertise of the enemy.

4. Make the enemy live up to its own book of rules. You can kill them with this, for they can no more obey their own rules than the Christian church can live up to Christianity.

5. Ridicule is man's most potent weapon.

6. A good tactic is one your people enjoy.

7. A tactic that drags on too long becomes a drag.

8. Keep the pressure on.

9. The threat is usually more terrifying than the thing itself.

10. The major premise for tactics is the development of operations that will maintain a constant pressure upon the opposition.

---

[35] Saul Alinsky, Rules for Radicals, A Practical Primer for Realistic Radicals, p.116

11. If you push a negative hard and deep enough, it will break through into its counter-side... every positive has its negative.

12. The price of a successful attack is a constructive alternative.

13. Pick the target, freeze it, personalize it, and polarize it.

What is the goal? How far do they plan to go in the reshaping of the USA? The answer is not clear, but the following three quotes might answer the questions.

"In this book we are concerned with how to create mass organizations to seize power and give it to the people; to realize the democratic dream of equality, justice, peace.... "Better to die on your feet than to live on your knees.' This means revolution."[36]

"Radicals must be resilient, adaptable to shifting political circumstances, and sensitive enough to the process of action and reaction to avoid being trapped by their own tactics and forced to travel a road not of their choosing."[37]

"A Marxist begins with his prime truth that all evils are caused by the exploitation of the proletariat by the capitalists. From this he logically proceeds to the revolution to end capitalism, then into the third stage of reorganization into a new social order of the dictatorship of the

---

[36] Saul Alinsky, Rules for Radicals, A Practical Primer for Realistic Radicals, p.3.
[37] Saul Alinsky, Rules for Radicals, A Practical Primer for Realistic Radicals, p.6.

proletariat, and finally the last stage -- the political paradise of communism."[38]

These eight levels of control must be obtained before you are able to create a socialist state:

Healthcare – Control healthcare to control the people.

Poverty – Increase the poverty level as high as possible: poor people will not fight back if you provide everything for them.

Debt – Increase the debt to an unsustainable level. Increase taxes to pay the debt. This produces more poverty.

Gun Control – Remove the ability for people to defend themselves from the government. Create a police state.

Welfare – Take control of every aspect of people's lives (Food, Housing, and Income)

Education – Take control of what people read, hear, and what they learn in school.

Religion – Remove God from government and schools

Class Warfare – Divide the people into "the wealthy" and "the poor." This causes more discontent makes it easier to take (Tax) the "wealthy" with the support of the poor.

This strategy worked because it is so far removed from Christianity. We couldn't believe it was possible. We were blinded to it and in denial.

As we reflect on the past 40+ years, I believe it is clear *Rules for Radicals* defined and shaped the current political culture. The common thread flowing through the eight levels of

---

[38] Saul Alinsky, Rules for Radicals, A Practical Primer for Realistic Radicals, p.10.

control is the stripping away of personal responsibility and creating a culture of dependency on the federal government.

How can we possibly defeat this plan? By the power of God! We must unite as the body of Jesus Christ here on earth, because through Him all things are possible. We must work to advance God's kingdom on earth.

We don't need the concepts outlined in *Rules for Radicals* to win this battle. The truth is on our side, found in our owners' manual. That manual is called "the *Bible.*"

✝

In those days there was no king in Israel; everyone did what was right in his own eyes.

(Judges 21:25)

Chapter 8

First Steps

So, how do we begin? We study how our great leaders gained wisdom from the "owners' manual" for life, the Bible, and its Author. They successfully led us out of very dark days on their "watch."

No other president has dealt with Abraham Lincoln's challenges. Many of us consider him one of the world's great leaders. During difficult times he said:

"I have been driven many times upon my knees by the overwhelming conviction that I had nowhere else to go. My own wisdom and that of all about me seemed insufficient for that day."

— Abraham Lincoln

We should follow Mr. Lincoln's lead and go to our knees in prayer for God's wisdom, direction and strength. No human being is capable of fixing our problems and returning the nation to one blessed by God.

It begins with me. Then you, and everyone reading this book. Once the Christian family is engaged, we need to take the message to the streets as disciples of Jesus Christ.

Throughout the Bible we are told to repent and turn back to God and He will forgive us our sins. This applies to individuals, churches, and nations. Our mission is to spread the gospel of Jesus Christ and to "occupy" until Jesus returns. This certainly doesn't imply restricting our beliefs only to the inside of the church. We are to let our light shine and shout it from the rooftops.

For whatever was written in earlier times was written for our instruction, so that through perseverance and the encouragement of the Scriptures we might have hope.

(Romans 15:4)

The churches should not begin endorsing candidates for any political office or siding with a political party. However churches should be teaching their membership how they should go about determining who to vote for.

It can only be logical to call on godly men and women to start reaching again for the spiritual concepts which made America great, because Jesus is the same yesterday, today and forever.

For, "...The grass withers, and the flower falls off, but the word of the Lord endures forever"

(Romans 1:24-25)

Abraham Lincoln wrote and delivered some of the greatest speeches in our country's history. They are still relevant, today. This speech was delivered on August 17, 1858 in the little town of Lewistown, Illinois:

[regarding the framers of the Declaration of Independence] "These communities, by their representatives in old Independence Hall, said to the whole world of men: "We hold these truths to be self evident: that all men are created equal; that they are endowed by their Creator with certain unalienable rights; that among these are life, liberty and the pursuit of happiness." This was their majestic interpretation of the economy of the Universe. This was their lofty, and wise, and noble understanding of the justice of the Creator to His creatures. Yes, gentlemen, to all His creatures, to the whole great family of man. In their enlightened belief, nothing stamped with the Divine image and likeness was sent into the world to be trodden on, and degraded, and imbruted by its fellows. They grasped not only the whole race of man then living, but they reached forward and seized upon the farthest posterity. They erected a beacon to guide their children and their children's children, and the countless myriads who should inhabit the earth in other ages. Wise statesmen as they were, they knew the tendency of prosperity to breed tyrants, and so they established these great self-evident truths, that when in the distant future some man, some faction, some interest, should set up the doctrine that none but rich men, or none but white men, were entitled to life, liberty and the pursuit of happiness, their posterity might look up again to the Declaration of Independence and take courage to renew the battle which their fa-

> thers began—so that truth, and justice, and mer-
> cy, and all the humane and Christian virtues
> might not be extinguished from the land; so that
> no man would hereafter dare to limit and cir-
> cumscribe the great principles on which the
> temple of liberty was being built."

\- Abraham Lincoln
[emphasis mine]

Read the speech again. Let it sink in! That is where our country is, right now. It is happening. The evil forces we are battling seek to extinguish all the human and Christian virtues from our land. And we the Body of Christ, His Church must repent and take up the Cross to save this nation.

In my opinion, the most perfect speech uttered by mortal man was delivered on the battlefield at Gettysburg. Millions of children learn it in school and even now Ken Burns a filmmaker is encouraging all Americans to memorize the speech. On that day, Abraham Lincoln spoke these revered words:

> "Four score and seven years ago our fathers brought forth on this continent a new nation, conceived in Liberty, and dedicated to the proposition that all men are created equal.

> Now we are engaged in a great civil war, testing whether that nation, or any nation so conceived and so dedicated, can long endure. We are met on a great battlefield of that war. We have come to dedicate a portion of that field, as a final resting place for those who here gave

their lives that that nation might live. It is altogether fitting and proper that we should do this.

But, in a larger sense, we can not dedicate -- we can not consecrate -- we can not hallow -- this ground. The brave men, living and dead, who struggled here, have consecrated it, far above our poor power to add or detract. The world will little note, nor long remember what we say here, but it can never forget what they did here. It is for us the living, rather, to be dedicated here to the unfinished work which they who fought here have thus far so nobly advanced. It is rather for us to be here dedicated to the great task remaining before us -- that from these honored dead we take increased devotion to that cause for which they gave the last full measure of devotion -- that we here highly resolve that these dead shall not have died in vain -- that this nation, under God, shall have a new birth of freedom -- and that government of the people, by the people, and for the people, shall not perish from the earth." [emphasis mine]

- Abraham Lincoln
November 19, 1863

We are in a battle right now for this nation, trying to ensure the government of the people, by the people, for the people, shall not perish from the earth.

Put on the full armor of God, so that you will be able to stand firm against the schemes of the devil.

(Ephesians 6:11)

The time to act is now, and – as with every initiative – we must begin with a vision:

Vision for the USA

God's kingdom on earth growing, Americans once again embracing Him as the foundation of our lives, and He is honored in all bodies of government.

✝

Build Your Kingdom Here

Come set Your rule and reign
in our hearts again.
Increase in us we pray.
Unveil why we're made.
Come set our hearts ablaze with hope
like wildfire in our very souls.
Holy Spirit, come invade us now.
We are Your church.
We need Your power in us.
Build Your kingdom here.
Let the darkness fear.
Show Your mighty hand.
Heal our streets and land.
Set Your church on fire.
Win this nation back.
Change the atmosphere.
Build Your kingdom here.
We pray.[39]

---

[39] Rend Collective, *Build Your Kingdom Here*

✟

Preach the Word

I solemnly charge you in the presence of God and of Christ Jesus, who is to judge the living and the dead, and by His appearing and His kingdom: preach the word; be ready in season and out of season; reprove, rebuke, exhort, with great patience and instruction. For the time will come when they will not endure sound doctrine; but wanting to have their ears tickled, they will accumulate for themselves teachers in accordance to their own desires, and will turn away their ears from the truth and will turn aside to myths. But you, be sober in all things, endure hardship, do the work of an evangelist, fulfill your ministry.

(2 Timothy 4:1-5)

But false prophets also arose among the people, just as there will also be false teachers among you, who will secretly introduce destructive heresies, even denying the Master who bought them, bringing swift destruction upon themselves. Many will follow their sensuality, and because of them the way of the truth will be maligned; and in their greed they will exploit you with false words; their judgment from long ago is not idle, and their destruction is not asleep.

(2 Peter 2:1-3)

Chapter 9

The Critical Time

Before we start thinking about the next steps, it is critical we establish values to guide us as a Christian body. We must be seen as loving in all we do, or our words won't mean anything to the secular culture. The media will destroy our efforts. They will throw everything they have at us. By God's grace we will prevail if we are true to Him in all things.

Values

1. **Evangelism**

   ...Go therefore and make disciples of all the nations, baptizing them in the name of the Father and the Son and the Holy Spirit, teaching them to observe all that I commanded you; and lo, I am with you always, even to the end of the age. (Matthew 28:19-20)

2. **Love**

   'YOU SHALL LOVE THE LORD YOUR GOD WITH ALL YOUR HEART, AND WITH ALL YOUR SOUL,

*AND WITH ALL YOUR MIND.' This is the great
and foremost commandment. The second is like it,
'YOU SHALL LOVE YOUR NEIGHBOR AS
YOURSELF.' On these two commandments depend
the whole Law and the Prophets.* (Matthew 22:37-
40)

3. **Forgiveness**
*"Lord, how often shall my brother sin against me
and I forgive him? Up to seven times?" Jesus said to
him, "I do not say to you, up to seven times, but up
to seventy times seven."* (Matthew 18: 21-22)

4. **Non-Conformational**
*Then Jesus said to him, "Put your sword back into
its place; for all those who take up the sword shall
perish by the sword.* (Matthew 26:52)

5. **Be Subjective to Government**
*Every person is to be in subjection to the governing
authorities. For there is no authority except from
God, and those which exist are established by God.
Therefore whoever resists authority has opposed the
ordinance of God; and they who have opposed will
receive condemnation upon themselves.* (Romans
13:1-2)

6. **Honor God's Word**
*All Scripture is inspired by God and profitable for
teaching, for reproof, for correction, for training in
righteousness;* (Timothy 3:16)

7. **Glory of God**

Whether, then, you eat or drink or whatever you do, do all to the glory of God. (1 Corinthians 10:31)

Key Initiatives

1. **Facilitate Training for Christians:**
   a. Taking the Gospel of Jesus Christ to the streets
   b. Understanding the rightful role God's church should have in civil government
   c. Making informed decisions before voting
   d. Promoting a positive message (never attacking another person or candidate)
   e. Developing K-12 curricula based on the role of God in our country and our government

2. **Support Christians: Individuals, Companies and Their Products**

   a. Encourage and support candidates who are committed to the advancement of God's kingdom here on earth.

   There may not always be a perfect candidate, but go with the one you feel is most likely to stay the course for God. If the media is attacking a contender, you might want to learn more about him. In my opinion, the ideal candidate believes in:

   - Pro-life
   - Constitutional form of government
   - Strong defense
   - Smaller government
   - Individual gun rights

- Fiscal responsibility
- Biblical view of marriage
- Secure U.S. borders
- Flat income tax
- Personal accountability
- Term limits for members of Congress

   b. Watch news networks which accurately report the events of the day

   c. Watch programs and buy from companies which promote a godly culture

3. **Pray for**

   a. Our leaders to repent and seek God's wisdom

   b. Christian candidates to seek office at all levels

   c. Smaller government with values promoting responsibility

   d. Our military to be guided by the spirit of God and kept safely in His arms

   e. A return to a court system which respects the Constitution and enforces laws accordingly

   f. A return to valuing all human life and a repeal of Roe v. Wade

   g. Churches to repent and preach the full gospel of Jesus Christ

The process of change within the Churches – to get them to accept civil responsibility – is no small task. After all, we have held back from participation for years!

Changing misconceptions to truth is always difficult. Still, God is speaking to many people today, and together we can make a mighty impact.

As a fellow citizen of the United States I ask everyone do these five things immediately:

1. Register to vote.
2. Apply for permanent absentee ballot where it is possible
3. Educate yourselves and others regarding candidates and issues using voter guides from the Christian Coalition
4. Vote in every election
5. Get involved in the GOTV (Get Out The Vote) campaign at election time

"When people ask you how you are going to vote in any upcoming election, your answer shouldn't be, "I'm going to vote with this side" or "I'm going to vote with that side." Your answer ought to be, "I'm voting with God because He has His own side. I am going to vote for the party, person, or platform that best represents God's values to advance His kingdom." ....

"One of the great tragedies in the church of Jesus Christ today is we have lost much of our ability and authority as an influence to others. We have lost this because we have divided and aligned ourselves with the politics of men. Rather than the power from and allegiance to a whole other King and kingdom, believers have taken sides with the two political parties. Believers have allowed political expedience to override the kingdom of God."

"God has not given His allegiance to any party. His allegiance belongs to Himself, His word, principles, and truth. As a follower of Jesus Christ, you represent His kingdom as well in whatever political capacity you choose to position yourself."[40]

And we should always remember our charter:

Then Jesus came to them and said, "All authority in heaven and on earth has been given to me. Therefore go and make disciples of all nations, baptizing them in the name of the Father and of the Son and of the Holy Spirit, and teaching them to obey everything I have commanded you. And surely I am with you always, to the very end of the age."

(Matthew 28:18-20)

---

[40] Tony Evans, TonyEvans.org | KAFellowship.org

When Lincoln was asked if God was on the Union's side, Lincoln said what was important was whether the Union was on *God's* side.[41]

Seventy-eight percent of the people in the U.S. claim to be Christian[42]. What if we had 30% of the Christians praying for a spiritual awakening? Every day! What might happen! There would be 75 million people praying for the same thing every day. I believe it is possible and if so there will be a domino effect, and through God's power we can make this happen. Jesus said,

> *"... if two of you on earth agree about some-thing and pray for it, it will be done for you by my Father in heaven."*

> (Matthew 18:19)

> *... God cannot lie when he makes a promise, and he cannot lie when he makes an oath.*

> (Hebrews 6:18)

Let's make the next three years the years of prayer and repentance. If it is God's will, we'll be amazed by the positive changes which will occur.

Let's be remembered as the generation that turned back to God, repented and embraced His moral values.

The time of waiting for someone *else* to do some-thing is over. We must act now. Our generation must not pass without correcting the course of our nation.

---

[41] Joe L. Wheeler, Abraham Lincoln, a Man of Faith and Cour-age: Stories of Our Most Admired President

[42] http://religions.pewforum.org/reports, p. 1

"Many people want "God bless America" today. They just don't want "One nation under God." The issue is that you can't have one without the other.[43]

Together, with God's grace, we can make it "One Nation Under God" again!

---

[43] Tony Evans, TonyEvans.org | KAFellowship.org

✝

Love is patient, love is kind and is not jealous; love does not brag and is not arrogant, does not act unbecomingly; it does not seek its own, is not provoked, does not take into account a wrong suffered, does not rejoice in unrighteousness, but rejoices with the truth; bears all things, believes all things, hopes all things, endures all things.

(1 Corinthians 13:4-7)

"World events are moving very rapidly now. I pick up the Bible in one hand, and I pick up the newspaper in the other and I read almost the same words in the newspaper as I read in the Bible. It's being fulfilled every day around us."

- Billy Graham
July 2, 1962

Chapter 10

Christian Love

As we started this book looking at the problems we have in America we looked back to our Founding Fathers to understand their intent and their words to inspire us. It is appropriate to once again review the actions of George Washington to give us an example of how to demonstrate Christian love in our lives. For our efforts to restore this nation will only succeed through our demonstration of Christian love.

William J. Johnson describes the following event in his book George Washington the Christian.

Example of Christian Charity

"While encamped at Valley Forge one day a Tory who was well known in the neighborhood was captured and brought into camp. His name was Michael Wittman, and he was accused of having carried aid and information to the British in Philadelphia. He was taken to West Chester and there tried by court-martial. It was proved that he was a very dangerous man and that he had more than once attempted to do great harm to the American army. He was pronounced guilty of being a spy and sentenced to be hanged. On the evening of the day before that set for the execution, a strange old man appeared at Valley Forge. He was a small man with long, snow-white hair falling over his shoulders. His face, although full of kindliness, was sad-looking and thoughtful; his eyes, which were bright and sharp, were upon the ground and lifted only when he was speaking...

His name was announced.

"Peter Miller?" said Washington. "Certainly. Show him in at once."

"General Washington, I have come to ask a great favor of you," he said, in his usual kindly tones.

"I shall be glad to grant you almost anything," said Washington, "for we surely are indebted to you for many favors. Tell me what it is."

"I hear," said Peter, "that Michael Wittman has been found guilty of treason and that he is to be hanged at Turk's Head tomorrow. I have come to ask you to pardon him."

Washington started back, and a cloud came over his face.

"That is impossible," he said. "Wittman is a bad man. He has done all in his power to betray us. He has even offered to join the British and aid in destroying us. In these times we dare not be lenient with traitors; and for that reason I cannot pardon your friend."

"Friend!" cried Peter. "Why, he is no friend of mine. He is my bitterest enemy. He has persecuted me for years. He has even beaten me and spit in my face, knowing full well that I would not strike back. Michael Wittman is no friend of mine." Washington was puzzled. "And still you wish me to pardon him?" he asked. "I do," answered Peter. "I ask it of you as a great personal favor."

"Tell me," said Washington, with hesitating voice, "why is it that you thus ask the pardon of your worst enemy?" "I ask it because Jesus did as much for me," was the old man's brief answer. Washington turned away and went into another room. Soon he returned with a paper on which was written the pardon of Michael Wittman. "My dear friend," he said, as he placed it in the old man's hands, "I thank you for this example of Christian charity."[44]

Until Jesus returns, we are to demonstrate Christian love as George Washington and Peter Miller did in this situation. Turning the other cheek, forgiving and remaining calm is not easy. However, it is what Jesus commands. The Holy Spirit convicts the world as Jesus told us.

---

[44] William Johnson, George Washington, The Christian, kindle version loc. 1182

And He, when He comes, will convict the world concerning sin, and righteousness, and judgment; concerning sin, because they do not believe in Me; and concerning righteousness, because I go to the Father, and you no longer behold Me; and concerning judgment, because the ruler of this world has been judged.

(John 16:8-11)

When we speak the truth of the Gospel we will experience the hate of the world, which will give us the opportunity to show love to them. Loving one another is truly happening when it is shaped by the testimony of our truth, the truth of Jesus Christ which by the Spirit convicts the world of sin. When there is hate, there is opportunity to love. Ironically, the gospel message of Jesus Christ is the reason many in the world hate us. However, He is also the reason we keep loving them!

To solve these problems we must repent and accept the accountability to take action. Will you? My prayer is you will say "Yes" with a confidence provided by the Holy Spirit. Encourage others to join you. The time to act is now. This book helps explain the problems and suggest appropriate actions to take. Each person and church should develop a list of actions, but you are being urged to follow the values and principles presented. And remember to always turn to God's word for his direction, and pray for His wisdom.

Saving the USA is no small task. It can't be accomplished by a few dedicated individuals. It will take the entire Christian family of Jesus Christ. How can we get the entire family to wake up and say we have had enough? It begins with you and me. We must take up His cross today and begin working within our families, churches, communities and regions; spreading the Gospel of Jesus Christ and encouraging others to do the same.

Visit the website SavingTheUSA.com. Its purpose is to connect the Christian family around the common goal of "Saving the USA." Everyone is encouraged to go to the site and register as a supporter of the mission. Please ask others to join in!

We have time to impact the elections this year and to begin making a difference in the national culture. Change will take a long time, but make no mistake, God is with us and He will prevail.

Will you help make a difference for the future generations?

Please join us in prayer, before it is too late.

Please "Christians Unite! Saving the USA." God will light the path for us to follow. However, we must all remember our purpose in life is to bring glory to God in all things, not glory to us. Please share this book with your pastor and as many Christians as you know.

God bless you!

✝

'Our Father who is in heaven,
Hallowed be Your name.
'Your kingdom come.
Your will be done,
On earth as it is in heaven.
'Give us this day our daily bread.
'And forgive us our debts, as we also have for-
given our debtors.
'And do not lead us into temptation, but deliver
us from evil. For Yours is the kingdom and the
power and the glory forever. Amen.'

(Matthew 6:9-13)

✞

All the Poor and Powerless

"All the poor and powerless
And all the lost and lonely
All the thieves will come confess
And know that You are holy
And know that You are

And all will sing out
Hallelujah
And we will cry out
Hallelujah
All the hearts who are content
And all who feel unworthy
And all who hurt with nothing left
Will know that You are holy

And all will sing out
Hallelujah
And we will cry out
Hallelujah

Shout it
Go on scream it form the mountains
Go on and tell it to the masses
That He is God
We will sing out
Hallelujah
And we will cry out
Hallelujah"[45]

---

[45] All Sons and Daughters – from the album *Brokenness Aside*

God Bless You
and
God Bless the USA

About the Author

Ernest Skipper is a tenth generation American, retired corporate executive, past consultant, minister, husband, father and grandfather.

During his 37-year career at Caterpillar Inc. (a world-leading manufacturer) he held leadership positions in 10 countries including U.S., Brazil, England and Japan. As a champion for productivity, ethical leadership and personal accountability, he repeatedly led teams to achieve radical transformations and unheard of cost reductions.

His article, "Path to Bold Goal Achievement" was widely used within Caterpillar and many other organizations. He was a featured contributing author in Lou Tice's book *Cultures of Excellence Volume I.*

Saved by the Grace of God, Ernest Skipper is a passionate leader and continues to dedicate his life to expanding God's Kingdom on earth and encouraging His people to step into their rights and responsibilities to the Glory of God.

Ernest and Vanna, his wife, live in Indiana and have 4 children and 6 grandchildren.

To unite with other Christians in our *Saving the USA* mission, and join our mailing list, visit www.SavingTheUSA.com

About the
Cover Image

In the late 1800's rural communities would build a community church that was shared by the various denominations utilizing traveling ministers. One church like this was in St. John, Missouri where I grew up. The church is long gone, but the memories remain, and we were inspired to build this chapel to give tribute to those churches that served the communities and most importantly glorified God.

Our Roadside Christian Chapel is located on State Road 43 North, Battle Ground, Indiana and is open 24/7 to everyone wishing to have some quite time to think or pray. It is also available by reservation for small weddings (capacity of 12).

Please feel free to stop by anytime.

Roadside Christian Ministries
7807 St Rd 43 North
Battle Ground, IN 47920

Our Mission: To spread the word of God, emphasizing personal accountability that leads to salvation through Jesus Christ.

www.ingramcontent.com/pod-product-compliance
Lightning Source LLC
Chambersburg PA
CBHW060649030426
42337CB00017B/2518

"THE BRIGHT FUTURE THAT LIES AHEAD FOR THIS NATIO
WILL BE THE RESULT OF THE NEW AMERICAN REVOLUTIONAR
LIKE ERNEST SKIPPER, WHO HAS IDENTIFIED OUR PROBLEM
AND LENDS HIS LIFE, FORTUNE AND SACRED HONOR T
SEEING THAT WE, AS A NATION, WITH A MISSION FROM GO
FULFILL THAT MISSION."

– PASTOR BILLY FALLING, THE INTERNET CHURC

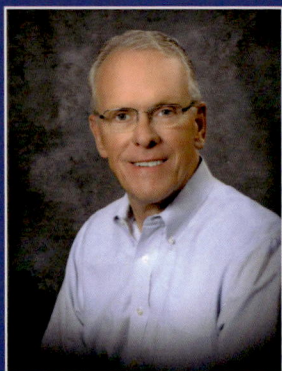

Ernest Skipper is a tenth
generation American,
retired corporate executive,
past consultant, minister,
husband, father and
grandfather. Saved by
the Grace of God, he is
a passionate leader and
continues to dedicate his
life to expanding God's
Kingdom on earth and
encouraging people to
step into their rights and
responsibilities to the Glory
of God.

"Christians Unite! Saving the USA" is a quick fo
hundred year walk through our country's Christ
heritage to the path we're on today.

This story begins in 1620 with the Pilgrims landing
Plymouth Rock. They came for the glory of God a
advancement of the Christian faith. Through ma
rough years, they faithfully fought for independen
a new government, and a constitution ensuring
religious freedom of all who would call this la
home. Patrick Henry said, at the signing of
Constitution, "It cannot be emphasized too stron
or too often that this great nation was founded, not
religionists, but by Christians; not on religions, but
the gospel of Jesus Christ!"

How sad that today we see God being systematica
removed from our government and our schools. T
very government that God ordained in 1789 n
targets Christian organizations and binds the hands
those who speak out for morality and life.

This book is a wake-up call and a call to action! T
final chapters lay out a vision and a plan to take up
cross and reestablish God's presence in our cult
and our government by 2020. And when we do,
have the promise of victory by God himself, "
seek first His kingdom and His righteousness, and
these things will be added to you." (Matthew 6:33)

By the grace of God and our actions, the 2020 visi
can become a reality. Unite with us.

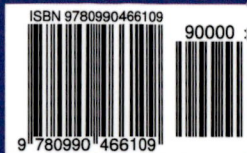

ISBN 9780990466109

90000

9 780990 466109